PICTURE THIS

A First Introduction to Paintings

FELICITY WOOLF

DOUBLEDAY
NEW YORK LONDON TORONTO SYDNEY AUCKLAND

Note to the reader

The words in **bold** are explained in the glossary on page 35.

PUBLISHED BY DOUBLEDAY
a division of Bantam Doubleday Dell Publishing Group, Inc.
666 Fifth Avenue, New York, New York 10103

Doubleday and the portrayal of an anchor with a dolphin
are trademarks of Doubleday, a division of
Bantam Doubleday Dell Publishing Group, Inc.

Published by arrangement with Hodder and Stoughton Ltd.

Library of Congress Cataloging-in-Publication Data
Woolf, Felicity.
Picture this: a first introduction to paintings / Felicity Woolf.
—1st ed.
p.   cm.
Includes index.
Summary: An introduction to Western painting from 1400 to 1950,
using famous works from major movements to illustrate the
development of Western art and explain basic concepts.
1. Painting—Themes, motives—Juvenile literature.   [1. Painting—
History.   2. Art appreciation.]   I. Title.
ND1146.W66   1990
750'.1'1—dc20   89-30459   CIP   AC
ISBN 0-385-41135-9
ISBN 0-385-41136-7 (lib. bdg.)

PRINTED IN ITALY
ALL RIGHTS RESERVED
FIRST EDITION IN THE UNITED STATES OF AMERICA, 1990
0590

Acknowledgments

My first experience of discussing old master paintings with children was gained at the National Gallery in London, where the highly successful children's program was developed by Anthea Peppin. Many of Anthea Peppin's ideas have been consciously or subconsciously incorporated into this book, and I would like to thank her most warmly. I also learned a great deal about making paintings accessible to children from Michael Cassin and James Heard, and from many of the free-lance staff who work with children at the National Gallery. Ann Whittaker, a London primary school teacher who uses paintings frequently with her pupils, and Barry Viney, who teaches at Dulwich College, both read the manuscript and offered me much encouragement. My husband, Fintan Cullen, studied the manuscript on numerous occasions and made many helpful suggestions. Lastly, I would like to thank Anna Sandeman, my editor at Hodder and Stoughton, who commissioned *Picture This*, and her assistant, Jenny Roberts, for their patience, advice, and enthusiasm.

Felicity Woolf

Contents

Introduction 6

Pictures and Writing: Paintings in Books 8

An Early Oil Painting 10

Painting on the Wall: A Renaissance Fresco 12

A Mythological Painting 14

The Artist and His Image: Two Self-portraits 16

Art for Everyone: Dutch Painting 18

Rich and Poor: Paintings from Eighteenth-Century Paris 20

From Sail to Steam: A World of Change 22

Making It Clear? Two Versions of a Story 24

The Impressionists and City Life 26

Color and Line: Painting and Expression 28

Dream and Fantasy: Surrealism 30

Action Painting 32

Glossary 35

Gallery List 37

Index 39

Picture Credits 40

Introduction

Although you probably paint and draw, you may not often look at and discuss other people's paintings. Looking at paintings can be interesting and fun, not only because they may be beautiful, but because they are part of history and can tell us about the past. They can tell us what people looked like, how they dressed, what was important to them, and what *they* considered to be beautiful.

You can find out a great deal about a painting by learning *how* to look at it and what questions to ask of it. It is rather like being a detective. For example, suppose you are looking at a **portrait**. (You do not need to learn a set of difficult words to enjoy looking at and talking about paintings. When you see a word in **bold**, like **portrait**, which may be new to you, you will find it explained in the Glossary on page 35.) You might decide instantly you like the face but want to know more about the person. Ask yourself, does the **sitter's** expression tell me anything? What about the clothes? Are they expensive? Where is the sitter? What does this setting tell me? Have a look at the portrait by Rubens on page 16, and ask these questions before you read about it. You will be surprised at how much you are able to work out for yourself.

Picture This is an introduction to the history of Western art, and all the pictures were painted in Europe and North America. Other parts of the world, such as Asia, South America, and Africa, are not included in this book. They have their own equally rich and varied art traditions, and each one needs a complete introduction of its own. I have chosen pictures painted between about 1400 and 1950. The book is arranged with the oldest paintings first and the most recent at the end. But you do not need to read the book from start to finish; you can dip into it wherever you like.

Only twenty-four paintings could be included out of many millions. I chose the paintings for various reasons. Most importantly, I think you will find them interesting. They also introduce you to some of the things that influence artists when they are working. Although artists may have special talents, they are always affected by the time and place in which they live. For instance, in many countries, up until the last century, artists' works were **commissioned**. This meant the artist had to paint what his or her patron — the person paying — wanted. The artist did not always have a free choice about what to paint or how to paint it.

Paintings made in the sixteenth century (page 12) often include perfect human figures, as it was commonly thought that the male body was the most beautiful form on earth. Paintings made in the Netherlands in the seventeenth century (page 18) were often small and cheap, and showed scenes of everyday life and the Dutch countryside. The Dutch were proud of their country and their way of life, and more people than ever bought paintings.

After the camera was invented in the last century, realistic painting seemed less special. Many artists felt that paintings should not try to be photographic. Instead, they could be simply an arrangement of lines and colors on a flat surface.

I hope this book will make you want to go and see the paintings. A list of the museums and galleries where they can be found is on page 37. However good, photographs of paintings can never be the same as seeing the real things. As well as tending to make the paint appear flat (oil paint can have a thick texture), and dulling the colors, photographs distort our sense of scale — all the paintings end up looking the same size. You should always note the **medium** and **support** of the painting and its actual size (measurements are in inches, with the height followed by the width). This information is printed near the illustrations.

Only two women artists are included in *Picture This*: Rachel Ruysch, a Dutch flower painter (page 19), and Berthe Morisot, an important French Impressionist painter (page 26). This is not because there were few women artists — there were many. But the women who worked as artists usually painted subjects such as flowers or made handwork, such as embroidery, and these types of paintings and crafts have been judged unimportant by historians. So, in a book which introduces some of the artists usually considered as the most famous in Western art, unfortunately very few women will be included.

You may notice that I have included no pictures painted after 1952. The closer you are to something, the more difficult it is to pick out the important parts. In the same way, looking back at paintings made recently, it is difficult to decide which ones will still seem interesting in the next century. "Painting" is no longer always a useful word; many artists now mix painting with other techniques. Some act out ideas or deliberately destroy their work after a few weeks or even days. These are some of the reasons why *Picture This* stops at 1952. I hope that what you learn from looking at earlier paintings will help you to make more sense of art that is being made now. You should certainly ask the same questions of it.

Pictures and Writing: Paintings in Books

This is a page from a book that was made entirely by hand in about 1400. This kind of book is called a **manuscript**. Manuscripts took a long time to make and were expensive to buy, so only rich people owned them. This one belonged to Philip the Bold, Duke of Burgundy. The page itself is **vellum**, which is stronger than paper. If you look carefully, you can see ruled lines that divide up the page into spaces for the picture, the writing (in French), and for the border decoration of leaves and stems.

The manuscript is a collection of stories about famous women. Thamaris was a painter, and this page in the manuscript is about her. The first letter of her name is large and elaborately decorated. You could draw a similar square around your own initial and decorate it. The picture, or **illumination**, shows Thamaris at work. Although she lived in Ancient Greece, she is shown as if she were an artist living in France in 1400, when the manuscript was made. Many manuscript illuminators were women.

Thamaris is painting a picture of Mary and her baby son, Jesus. The painting is on a wooden panel, which is supported on an **easel**. Thamaris is holding a **palette** in her left hand. Artists still use easels and palettes today. In the **foreground** is a table with spare brushes and colors in shells. Behind Thamaris, in the background, a young assistant is getting colors ready for the artist.

You could not buy ready-made paints in 1400, and every artist mixed colors in his or her workshop. This assistant is making blue, probably by grinding up the semiprecious stone lapis lazuli on a flat stone board. The fine **pigment** was then mixed with the **medium**, which for manuscript illuminations was egg white, egg yolk, or glue. Gold leaf was used on this page, in addition to colored pigments. Shapes cut from leaves of thinly beaten gold were fixed to the page with glue.

1. *Thamaris, the Most Noble Artist*
from Boccaccio,
Concerning Famous Women

Artist unknown
1403–4
13×9½ inches
Tempera and gold leaf on
vellum

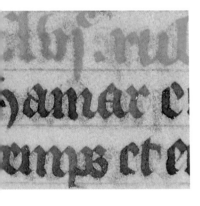

Detail from *Thamaris, the Most Noble Artist*. The first letter of Thamaris' name is enlarged and decorated to make it stand out.

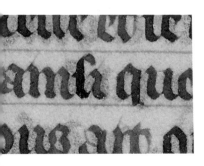

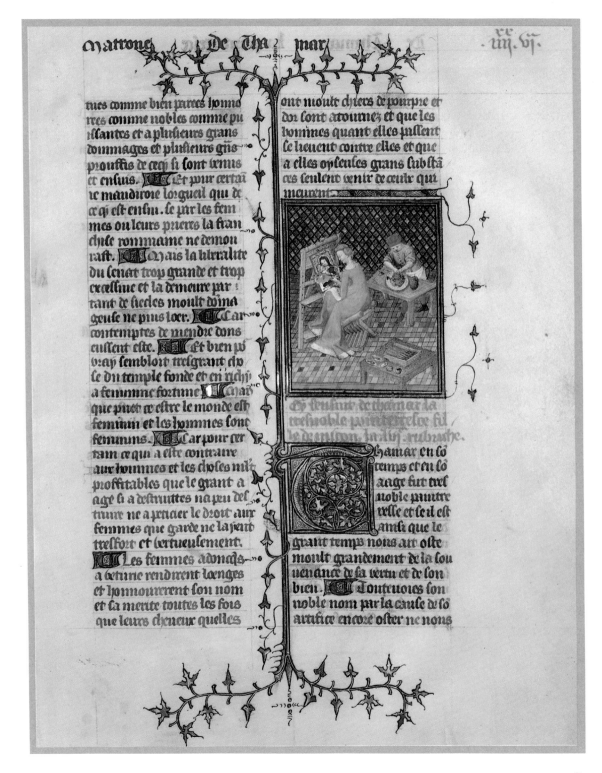

An Early Oil Painting

From about 1400, artists working in Flanders, now part of Belgium, became famous all over Europe. Their paintings were admired because they were very realistic. The artists included many tiny details, and also showed how colors change according to the light. In strong light, colors appear bright, while in shadow they are duller and tend to merge together. The artists mixed their **pigments** with oil. Oil paint can be put on in layers, so that the artist can build up deep colors.

This painting was probably made in Tournai, although it is not certain who painted it. Other paintings by an artist called Robert Campin are similar to this one. Campin had a workshop in the city, and one of the assistants he had trained may have painted it. It is a small **altarpiece**, made to be used at home for private prayer. The most important picture is in the middle and called *The Annunciation*. The scene is set in a house. The angel Gabriel, God's messenger, is on the left. He is telling Mary that God has chosen her to be the mother of His son, Jesus. The tiny baby who has flown through the window on the left is meant to be Jesus. Although this is a miraculous moment, everything in the lifelike room seems quiet and normal.

Detail from *A Triptych with the Annunciation in the Center*. The artist took care to make the view from Joseph's workshop realistic.

The room is just as it would have been in 1420. Can you find the firescreen that protects Mary from the fire, and the spiked candlestick to hold the candle in place? Can you work out how the shutters close, or does the painter himself seem a bit confused by them?

There are smaller **wings** hinged onto the sides of *The Annunciation*. These can be kept closed to protect the central picture. When the

altarpiece, or **triptych**, is open — as it is here
— the left wing shows a man and woman
kneeling in a garden. They probably
commissioned the altarpiece. On the right is
an old man sitting at a carpenter's bench. He is
Joseph, Mary's husband. Can you find his
carpenter's tools? Look at the windowsill. Can
you see the mouse trap he has made? It is
included to remind Christians that God sent
Jesus down to earth as a trap to catch the
Devil!

The artist may have painted his **self-portrait** in
the garden behind the two people kneeling by
the door.

*2. A Triptych with the
Annunciation in the
Center* (known as **The
Mérode Altarpiece)**

Ascribed to Robert
Campin
about 1425
center: 25¼×24⅞ inches;
wings: 25¼×10¾ inches
Oil on wood

Painting on the Wall: A Renaissance Fresco

This painting illustrates á line from Genesis, the first book in the Bible: "God created man in His own image." On the right God is giving life to Adam, the first man.

The Creation of Adam is only one small part of a huge ceiling, completely decorated with paintings. The ceiling is in the Sistine Chapel, built for Pope Sixtus IV in the 1470s in the Vatican palace in Rome. The Vatican is still the home of the Pope today. The Pope is the head of the Roman Catholic Church. It took about four years to paint the ceiling, and the work had to be done from scaffolding. Much of the time Michelangelo was positioned uncomfortably close to the ceiling.

The painting was done in **fresco**. Fresco is Italian for "fresh," and describes a way of painting directly onto wet plaster. The powdered **pigments** become part of the plaster as it dries. It is a cheap and fast method of painting, and is good for covering large areas such as walls and ceilings.

As Adam was thought to be the first man made by God, he looks completely perfect, like a kind of superman, ready to spring into heroic action. When Michelangelo was alive (1475–1564), the male body was considered the most beautiful form on earth. It was important for an artist to be able to draw men very well.

To practice this skill, Michelangelo made drawings of **life models** in his **studio**. He also dissected dead bodies, so that he could see the structure of the bones and muscles under the skin.

Michelangelo also studied **classical** sculptures of men, which had survived from Ancient Roman times. These sculptures were lifelike, but at the same time had perfect, superhuman bodies. Michelangelo's interest in Roman sculpture was shared by many people during his lifetime, a period known as the **Renaissance.**

The drawing on this page is probably of a life model. Can you see how the model's left leg moved and Michelangelo changed the outline? The right hand was at a difficult angle, so the artist drew it separately. In the fresco Adam is in the same **pose** as in the drawing. From this time up to the present day, artists have often made drawings to work out their ideas before starting to paint.

3. The Creation of Adam

Michelangelo
about 1511
110¼×227½ inches
Fresco

4. Study for Adam

Michelangelo
about 1511
7½×10¼ inches
Red chalk on paper

A Mythological Painting

This painting is about the hunter Actaeon and the goddess Diana. Actaeon, on the left, has been out hunting with friends. While they rest during the heat of the day, Actaeon wanders into the woods to find shade. Unfortunately, he stumbles upon the place where the goddess Diana is bathing with her women helpers. Diana has vowed never to have anything to do with men, and is extremely angry when Actaeon sees her naked. She splashes water at Actaeon and where the drops fall antlers sprout from his head. He gradually turns into a stag, until his own hounds catch his scent and give chase. They bring him down and tear him to death.

Titian has painted the moment when Actaeon accidentally discovers Diana. Diana is sitting on the right. Her arm is raised and she wears a crescent moon on her head. The Ancient Greeks (who called her Artemis) and Romans thought of her as a goddess of the moon. The painting was made during the **Renaissance**, when many people were interested in **classical** myths. Myths are traditional stories, often about ancient gods and goddesses. They sometimes explain part of the natural world, such as the moon and the sun, or thunder and lightning. *Diana and Actaeon* was **commissioned** by King Philip II of Spain. He liked paintings that included naked women, but because the women were from mythology, and not real, the paintings were not considered offensive.

Diana and Actaeon is painted on **canvas**. Paintings on canvas can be rolled up and are easy to transport. This was important for Titian, as he often sent paintings to places far from Venice, where he lived. Canvas became a popular **support** during the sixteenth century and gradually replaced the use of wooden panels.

Venetian painting was famous for the variety and good quality of its colors. Titian used bright, contrasting colors. He did not make many drawings before he began to paint, but made a rough **sketch** on the canvas. Sometimes he changed parts of his **composition** as he went along. The surface of Titian's paintings is sometimes rough and uneven. The paint can be thick and show the marks of the brush, because it has been put on quickly and not smoothed and blended. Titian was one of the first artists to use oil paint in this way.

5. *Diana and Actaeon*

Titian
1556–59
74×80 inches
Oil on canvas

Detail from *Diana and Actaeon*. Titian was skilled at painting different textures, such as fur and fabric.

The Artist and His Image: Two Self-portraits

Nowadays we like to have photographs to remind us of special moments in our lives. Before the invention of photography, rich people had **portraits** painted of themselves and their relatives. Can you guess why this **double portrait** was painted? One clue is the honeysuckle behind the couple. This is a flower associated with love. Look how the man and woman are holding hands. The man points to the ring on his wife's right hand. This is a marriage portrait, painted soon after their wedding.

Although the painting is more than three hundred and fifty years old, we know the identities of the couple. The man is the artist Peter Paul Rubens, and the woman is Isabella Brandt. They were married in 1609. Rubens painted this portrait himself, so it is a **self-portrait** as well as a marriage portrait. From this picture would you guess that Rubens was a painter? Rubens and Isabella Brandt are dressed in the elegant and lavish Spanish style, fashionable in Antwerp where they lived. You would hardly wear clothes like this for painting! Rubens wants to show that he is a wealthy and successful gentleman, and not someone who makes a living by using his hands and getting dirty in a **studio**.

Rubens went on to be one of the most successful and famous artists in Europe. He was court painter in Antwerp and was sent on diplomatic missions to Spain and England. Rubens also valued family life and often painted his wife and their children. This painting tells us about two sides of his life — public and private.

6. Rubens and Isabella Brandt in the Honeysuckle Bower

Peter Paul Rubens
1609
70×53½ inches
Oil on canvas

7. Self-portrait, Aged 63

Rembrandt
1669
33⅞×27¾ inches
Oil on canvas

The Dutch artist Rembrandt painted an unusually large number of self-portraits. About fifty are still known today. They show the artist at every stage of his life, from youth to old age. This one was done when Rembrandt was in his sixties. The portrait does not show a confident gentleman, but a simply dressed, slightly worried elderly man.

Rembrandt worked in Amsterdam and as a young man was very successful. But then his style of painting, with few colors and thick encrusted paint, went out of fashion, and in 1656 he went bankrupt. This self-portrait was completed thirteen years later.

As far as we know, the portrait does not celebrate a special occasion, as Rubens' marriage portrait does. Rembrandt's paintings of different stories, often from the Bible, were famous for the way in which the artist showed people's feelings and reactions. Rembrandt may have used his self-portraits to explore different ways of painting the human face, with its range of expressions. Here he has used few colors. The figure seems to loom out of the darkness. Light falls only on the face and hands, the most expressive and individual parts of the body.

Art for Everyone: Dutch Painting

The Netherlands became independent at the beginning of the seventeenth century. The Dutch were proud of their country, which they had to defend continually against flooding from the sea. The sea also brought wealth to the nation. The Dutch used their large fleet to trade with distant countries. Many people had enough spare money to buy paintings to decorate their homes. New kinds of paintings became popular, especially **landscapes, genre paintings,** and **still lifes**.

The landscapes often show the flat, open Dutch countryside, with much of the painting taken up by cloud-filled sky. This is a view of an avenue of trees planted in 1664, outside the town of Middelharnis on the island of Overflakkee. The tallest trees in the **foreground** divide up the painting into equal sections; everything seems calm and ordered. Can you see the large church tower in the background? On the right, young trees are growing; with time and care, they will replace the large trees in the avenue.

8. *The Avenue,*
Middelharnis

Meyndert Hobbema
1689
40¾×55½ inches
Oil on canvas

9. *The Milkmaid*

Jan Vermeer
about 1660
17⅞×16⅛ inches
Oil on canvas

The Milkmaid shows a completely ordinary moment in any household — a woman pouring milk into a bowl. The house is in Delft. The tiles, which you can see just above the floor, were made there. The artist, Jan Vermeer, has seen and recorded everything in the room with the accuracy of a camera lens. The table, basket, bread, jug, and bowl appear heavy and solid, as if you could pick them out of the painting. Do you remember another painting of a room? Turn back to *The Annunciation* on page 11. That painting was made not very far from Delft, but nearly two hundred and fifty years earlier. Vermeer's picture continues the tradition of detailed realistic painting, typical of artists working in Northern Europe.

———————◆———————

Flower paintings were also popular in the Netherlands. They usually showed varieties of flowers that were expensive and highly prized. Although the paintings seem realistic, not all of the flowers shown bloom at the same time. The artist Rachel Ruysch probably kept a book of drawings of different flowers. She may have copied these and "arranged" them in her **composition**. Picked flowers quickly wither and die, and it may be that the Dutch flower paintings were to remind people of the shortness of life. Many women worked as flower painters. The idea that flowers were a suitably "ladylike" subject for women to paint lasted until at least the end of the nineteenth century.

10. *Flowers in a Vase*

Rachel Ruysch
about 1705
22½×17⅛ inches
Oil on canvas

19

Rich and Poor: Paintings from Eighteenth-Century Paris

What can you learn about this lady from her **portrait**? Look at her clothes, her face, her hands, the furniture, and all the things that are scattered about the room. The lady wears a green silk dress, decorated with lace, pink ribbons, and roses. A whole bouquet of spring flowers is attached to her shoulder. She has a flawless white skin and tiny feet! There are books and music and a pet spaniel. There is a mirror behind the lady. Can you work out what it reflects? It shows the back of the **sitter's** graceful head and neck, and gives us a glimpse of the other side of the room, where there is a bookcase and a clock. This reflection adds to our impression of a grand and spacious room, full of expensive furniture. Would you like to be in the room? Do you like the way the colors and shapes all go together?

This is a portrait of Madame de Pompadour, who lived at the court of Louis XV in Paris, as the King's mistress. Madame de Pompadour **commissioned** many paintings and took an active part in deciding how her apartments should be decorated. This picture tells us a lot about her life at court. It was a life that did not involve work, but only idleness, beauty, and pleasure.

11. *Madame de Pompadour*

François Boucher
1756
79⅛×61¾ inches
Oil on canvas

Of course, someone had to do the work! While some artists, such as François Boucher, showed the life of the courtiers, others painted the servants. The kitchen maid in Chardin's painting is scraping turnips, ready for cooking. Apart from the vegetables, pots and pans, and knives for peeling and chopping, the artist has included no information about the world inhabited by the maid. Does the dark background suggest anything about her life? Resting on her sofa, Madame de Pompadour seems delicate and graceful and lost in pleasant thoughts. The maid is heavy and round-shouldered by comparison. Her hands are red and raw from hard work. What do you think she is thinking about?

You may think she is tired and bored with her work, and wishing she were in the restful position of a lady like Madame de Pompadour. But this would be looking at the painting from a modern point of view. We know that in paintings of servants and tradespeople, like this one, Chardin was showing that everyone has a job to do and should keep to his or her position in society, however lowly. This was a commonly held belief at the time.

If you turn back to *The Milkmaid* on page 18, you can see another working woman. Chardin was very much interested in Dutch **genre paintings** and looked at many to get ideas for his own work.

12. *The Turnip Scraper*

Jean-Baptiste-Siméon
Chardin
1738
18¼×14¾ inches
Oil on canvas

From Sail to Steam: A World of Change

In 1838 a huge ship with ninety-eight guns was towed up the Thames River to the docks at Rotherhithe in London. There she was broken up. Although the ship, the *Fighting Téméraire*, had had a great career, taking part in the Battle of Trafalgar, sail power was nearing its end. From now on, boats would be powered by steam.

The artist Turner probably saw the *Fighting Téméraire* as she was being towed up the river by a tugboat. He felt that this last journey would make an interesting subject for a painting. On one half of the **canvas** Turner painted a bright orange-red sunset. The clouds at the top of the sky, touched with yellow and orange, are reflected in the water at the bottom of the painting. Although a sunset can be very beautiful, it is also a melancholy time of day — it marks the end of something. So, why do you think Turner chose to paint the *Fighting Téméraire* at sunset?

13. *The "Fighting Téméraire" Tugged to Her Last Berth to Be Broken Up, 1838*

Joseph Mallord William Turner
1838, exhibited 1839
35¾×48 inches
Oil on canvas

You have looked at the range of colors on one side of the picture; now look at the left-hand side of the painting. Can you find the moon, which is rising as the sun sets? Turner uses black for the dirty metal tugboat. The dark squat shape of the tug contrasts with the white and gray of the elegant *Fighting Téméraire*, which looks almost like a ghost ship. Turner was one of the first artists in England to paint new machinery. Do you think he preferred the tugboat to the old sailing ship?

For parts of *The "Fighting Téméraire", Tugged to Her Last Birth to Be Broken Up, 1838,* Turner used very runny oil paint. As you can see in the **foreground**, this thin paint gives a good impression of still, smooth water. Turner was used to working with thin **washes** of color, because he also painted pictures in **watercolor**. Working on paper, sometimes with very few colors, Turner created brilliant effects.

———◆———

The other picture shown here is a watercolor of Venice in Italy, where the sunlight is particularly bright. The buildings are painted in a single color and stand out clearly against the early morning sun. You can compare this view of a city with the London skyline on the right in *The "Fighting Téméraire," Tugged to Her Last Birth to Be Broken Up, 1838.*

14. *Looking East from the Giudecca: Early Morning*

Turner
1819
8¾×11¼ inches
Watercolor on paper

Making It Clear? Two Versions of a Story

Ophelia went mad with grief after her father's death and drowned herself. Her tragic story comes from William Shakespeare's play *Hamlet*. When you are watching the play, you do not see Ophelia drown; you only hear about her death. Millais turned the description from the play into this painting.

Shakespeare said Ophelia died at a place where a willow tree grew low over a stream. She slipped from the tree as she tried to hang garlands of flowers on the branches. To make

his painting as much like the description as possible, Millais set up his **easel** on the bank of the Hogsmill River in Surrey, where a willow tree and many varieties of wild flowers grew. Painting in the open air was not easy. Millais was chased by a bull, an angry farmer, and two swans!

Millais painted the riverbank first and left space for Ophelia. His friend Elizabeth Siddall, who was also an artist, agreed to **model** for Ophelia. She lay in a bath full of water, kept

15. *Ophelia*

John Everett Millais
1852
30×44 inches
Oil on canvas

warm by lamps underneath. Unfortunately, she still caught cold and Millais had to pay for a doctor.

Millais belonged to a group of artists called the Pre-Raphaelite Brotherhood, formed in 1848. These artists admired old paintings made before the time of Raphael, who died in 1520. They thought those paintings were easy to understand, sincere and well made. They noticed that the colors in some paintings from the fifteenth century kept their brilliance, despite the fact that oil paint tends to darken with age. Like the artist who painted *The Annunciation* **altarpiece** in about 1425 (see page 11), Millais first covered his canvas with a white **ground**. Any color put on top of white appears bright. A dark ground tends to darken

other colors. You can try this out for yourself by painting the same color first on white paper, then on black.

In the National Gallery in London there is another picture of Ophelia. If you turn the book on its side, you can see that the artist began by drawing a vase of exotic flowers. He did not copy the flowers; he made them up out of his imagination. Then the flowers reminded him of Ophelia's death. The artist turned the paper on its side and drew in her face, in **profile**.

Now the outline of the vase looks like a rocky landscape, although nothing is very clear. Redon did not want the picture to look like a photograph of the place where Ophelia died. He wanted it to be more like a fantasy, a kind of dream.

This picture is not an oil painting. It was done in **pastel**. Pastels give a soft, fuzzy effect. Compare this pastel picture with Millais' oil painting. Which do you prefer?

16. *Ophelia Among the Flowers*

Odilon Redon
1905–8
25¼×35⅞ inches
Pastel on card

The Impressionists and City Life

In 1874 a group of young artists exhibited their paintings together in Paris. Some people who did not like their work called them "Impressionists." Can you see why?

The paintings shocked people because some of them looked like rough **sketches** rather than finished paintings. The Impressionists, as they became known, painted like this because they believed it was the best way to show how colors change according to the light. You can see this most clearly in the painting by Berthe Morisot of a servant in the dining room. Morisot painted part of the room brightly lit by sunlight, which reflects off the maid's apron, the floor, the table, and other shiny surfaces in the room. The farther you hold the painting away from you, the clearer the effect. You could compare the painting with *The Milkmaid* by Vermeer on page 18. Which painting is more successful at showing light in a room?

Because they were interested in studying sunlight, the Impressionists often painted

17. *In the Dining Room*

Berthe Morisot
1886
24⅛×19⅝ inches
Oil on canvas

18. *The Seine at Asnières (The Skiff)*

Pierre-Auguste Renoir
about 1879
28×36¼ inches
Oil on canvas

outside. This was difficult for Berthe Morisot, as respectable women could not go out alone and wander freely in Paris. As a result, Morisot often painted places or people near at hand, such as this serving girl in her own dining room.

＊

Renoir had no such difficulties, and his picture of two people rowing a boat on a hot summer's day was probably painted outside, on the riverbank. The paint has been put on in dabs and dashes that go in different directions and suggest the shape of the leaves and the movement of the water. The painting is very bright. Renoir has put two contrasting colors, orange and blue, next to each other, with the result that both seem even brighter. Renoir believed that this was the best way to paint the effect of light on water and create the feeling of a warm, lazy day. Do you agree?

＊

Degas also belonged to the Impressionist group. He always painted in his **studio**, not outside in front of his subject. In *La La at the Cirque Fernando* the paint is put on smoothly. Many of Degas' paintings show different

entertainments in Paris — the ballet, horse racing, and here the circus. The acrobat, La La, has been hauled high into the air by a rope. She holds the end of the rope in her teeth. Degas shows her nearly at the roof, with the lights from below shining on her ribs and stomach.

19. *La La at the Cirque Fernando, Paris*

Hilaire-Germaine-Edgar
Degas
1879
46×30½ inches
Oil on canvas

Color and Line: Painting and Expression

The Impressionists (page 26) used rough brushstrokes and bright colors to suggest the way we see the natural world. Van Gogh, a generation younger than the Impressionists, used color and the shape and thickness of painted lines and forms to express his feelings about whom or what he was painting.

This is a **self-portrait** of the artist, painted while he was in a mental hospital. The swirling lines of color in the background do not describe anything real, but give an idea of the turmoil in van Gogh's mind. The angular face, beard, and jacket are painted with bold, thick strokes of paint. One of the reasons van Gogh made his paintings so rough in texture was so they would be as different as possible from photographs. Photography, which gives an instantly realistic picture, was just becoming popular. Van Gogh wrote letters to his brother explaining the way he painted:

> *Those photographic portraits wither much sooner than we ourselves do, whereas the painted portrait is a thing which is felt, done with love or respect for the human being that is portrayed.*

Do you agree with van Gogh? Do you like paintings of people more than photographs?

20. *Self-portrait*

Vincent van Gogh
1889
25½×21¼ inches
Oil on canvas

Despite van Gogh's dislike of photography, his painting is still similar to the way we all see the shape of a man's shoulders and head. In Pablo Picasso's picture *Weeping Woman*, the artist paints something different. We know this is a woman's head — we can see a hat, long hair, eyes, the frame of a pair of glasses, a mouth, and hands. But what has happened?

The face has not been shown as if the artist were looking at it from one position. Instead we can see a side view, which should include just one eye, but which in fact includes two. Many of the lines and shapes seem to be several things at once — the small driplike shapes falling from the eyes are tears, splinters of glass, and fingernails. Even the eyes look like circles of broken glass from a pair of spectacles. Can you see other shapes in the painting that can be seen as two things?

Picasso could have made the head look normal, but he chose not to. He felt the garish colors, the thick lines, and different but combined views of the face made the woman look more grief-stricken. From the fifteenth century, artists had believed that paintings should look realistic and should show things as the human eye sees them. Picasso was one of the first artists to question this belief.

21. *Weeping Woman*

Pablo Picasso
1937
23⅝×19¼ inches
Oil on canvas

Dream and Fantasy: Surrealism

What can you see in *The Horde*? On the right an apelike creature is running toward the crowd of shapes on the left. Some of these seem half human. We can make out hands, legs, and feet. It is not clear what is happening. Perhaps the biggest figure is trampling on the rest, or perhaps the darker-colored monsters are all attacking the brighter figure lying down. The artist has created the fear and the half-real world of a nightmare. Have you ever painted or described what you remember of a dream?

Max Ernst, who painted *The Horde*, belonged to a group of artists called the Surrealists. They began to work together in Paris in the 1920s. The Surrealists often painted their dreams. They believed that we are not completely aware of what controls our behavior.

Experiences from the past we think we have forgotten may still remain in our minds and affect us. Sometimes these experiences, and the feelings of fear or happiness that went with them, may be shown to us again in dreams. The Surrealists thought that artists should paint and draw these hidden experiences, which they felt were more important than the world or the reality we usually see and think about. They are called the Surrealists because their paintings go beyond reality.

Some of the Surrealists, including Max Ernst, invented new ways to make paintings, to help them get back to their lost experiences and feelings. To make *The Horde*, Ernst placed a **canvas** over a tangle of string, then scribbled on the canvas with a crayon. You can see the curved marks left by the string. The marks did not seem just a random pattern to Ernst. They suggested monsters, chasing or fighting. Ernst may have believed that in this way he was rediscovering a frightening experience he had had in the past, such as being lost or being terrified in a crowd.

22. *The Horde*

Max Ernst
1927
$18\frac{1}{8} \times 21\frac{5}{8}$ inches
Oil on canvas

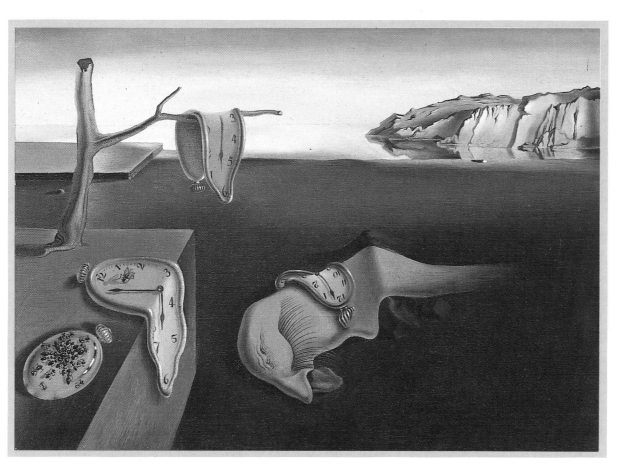

23. *The Persistence of Memory*

Salvador Dali
1931
9½×13 inches
Oil on canvas

The Persistence of Memory is another Surrealist painting. The landscape is realistic, yet what we see is beyond reality. It is dreamlike, and the strange shape in the middle of the barren landscape suggests a sleeping head. There are four clocks in the landscape, three of which are folded, as if they were soft, like leaves. We cannot say exactly what the painting is about. Perhaps the sleeping "man" is dreaming of the past.

The precisely drawn insects are traditionally linked with the passing of time, which leads to death. Sometimes Dutch flower painters included insects on the flowers in their paintings. Do you remember how these flowers may have suggested that nothing lasts very long? (See page 19.)

Salvador Dali, the artist, often makes new and strange connections between things — here, for example, a clock and a fly — and gives ordinary objects new qualities, as with the soft clocks. By doing this, he shocks us into thinking afresh about something, in this case time. Knowing that time is usually connected with what will happen in the future, Dali may be suggesting that the lingering effects of the past are in fact of greater importance.

Action Painting

This painting is different from any of the others we have looked at. The most obvious difference is that it is an **abstract painting**. Abstract painting is one of the most significant inventions of the twentieth century.

To make *Blue Poles* Pollock laid out a large canvas on the floor. He moved around the outside edges and dripped trails of wet paint onto the canvas from sticks that had been dipped into large pots of car paint. *Blue Poles: Number II* is one of Pollock's most famous "drip" paintings. The way in which this method, or action, of painting gives the finished work its particular character is one reason why this style is sometimes called action painting.

Action painting may seem a very haphazard way of painting — the stick brushes do not touch the canvas, and as the stick is waved quickly across the surface, the paint falls onto the work, rather than being carefully placed. Yet, if you look carefully at the thick layers of paint, you can see the **composition** is not disorganized. There is a limited number of colors spread across the canvas, and the eight upright poles, four in each half, create a pattern. Perhaps a useful way to describe the work is as an irregular web or pattern of color.

Why did Pollock paint like this? Like van Gogh (see page 28), Pollock felt that the invention of photography meant painting no longer needed to show the world realistically.

He agreed with the Surrealists (see page 30) that artists should instead try to show their most private feelings and experiences. With the "drip" technique, Pollock built up the painting as he went along. He found that this spontaneous method allowed him to find out how he felt as he worked.

Looking at a painting like *Blue Poles: Number II,* we cannot say exactly what Pollock was trying

to express — perhaps feelings of anger, fear, and confusion. Abstract painting differs from other types of painting because it can be fully understood only by the artist. For this reason many people do not like abstract art. Do you think you should be able to understand a painting quickly and easily? Or is it part of the fun of looking to suggest different meanings? Or is it enough to enjoy the colors and shapes and the way the artist has put on the paint?

Detail from *Blue Poles: Number II*. Pollock's "drip" technique built up a thick, layered texture.

24. *Blue Poles: Number II*

Jackson Pollock
1952
83×192 inches
Enamel and aluminium paint with glass on canvas

33

Glossary

abstract painting   a painting in which the lines and colors do not make a realistic picture

altarpiece   a religious painting, made to stand on the altar of a Christian church or chapel

ascribed to   thought to be by the named artist

canvas   a coarse, woven material on which artists can paint

classical   from Ancient Greece or Rome

commissioned   ordered and paid for by

composition   the way a painting is organized

double portrait   a **portrait** of two people

easel   a stand that holds the **support** ready for painting

foreground   in a realistic painting the space is divided into foreground, middle ground, and background. The foreground is the space nearest the viewer.

fresco   a method of painting on wet plaster

genre painting   a painting of everyday life

ground   the first layer of paint, which completely covers the **canvas** or wood

illumination   a picture in a **manuscript**

landscape   a painting of the countryside

life model   a person who **poses** in a **studio**, to be drawn by an artist

manuscript   a handwritten book or page

medium   the liquid with which the **pigment** is mixed

to model   to stay in a **pose** while someone draws or paints you

palette   a piece of wood with a thumbhole, used to hold colors needed for a painting

pastel   soft, colored chalk

pigment	a colored powder that gives paint its color	**support**	the surface on which the picture is painted, such as **canvas**
portrait	a painting that records a particular person	**tempera**	paint with a **medium** of egg white, egg yolk, glue, or water
pose	position		
to pose	to take up a position	**triptych**	an **altarpiece** in three parts, consisting of a central section and two **wings**
profile	a side view of a face		
Renaissance	a period in European history, from about 1400 to 1600, during which there was renewed interest in all aspects of life in Ancient Greece and Rome	**vellum**	paper made from animal skin
		wash	a thin, transparent layer of **watercolor**
self-portrait	a **portrait** by an artist of him or herself	**watercolor**	a method of painting, in which **pigments** are mixed with water and glue
sitter	the person who is the subject of a **portrait**		
sketch	a rough outline	**wings**	painted side doors that close over the central part of a **triptych**
still life	a painting of a group of objects, such as china, fruit, or flowers		
studio	an artist's workroom		

Gallery List

Cover: **The Cholmondeley Sisters,** (c. 1600-1610), anonymous 17th-Century British artist, Tate Gallery, London

1. **Thamaris, the Most Noble Artist,** folio 86 from Boccaccio, *Concerning Famous Women*, artist unknown (active c.1400), Bibliothèque Nationale, Paris

2. **A Triptych with the Annunciation in the Center** (known as **The Mérode Altarpiece), ascribed to** Robert Campin (1378/9–1444), the Metropolitan Museum of Art, New York, Cloisters Collection

3. **The Creation of Adam**, Michelangelo (1475–1564), Sistine Chapel, Vatican, Rome

4. **Study for Adam**, Michelangelo, the British Museum, London

5. **Diana and Actaeon**, Titian (c.1480–1576), Collection of the Duke of Sutherland, on loan to the National Gallery of Scotland, Edinburgh

6. **Rubens and Isabella Brandt in the Honeysuckle Bower**, Peter Paul Rubens (1577–1640), Alte Pinakothek, Munich

7. **Self-portrait, Aged 63**, Rembrandt (1606–69), the National Gallery, London

8. **The Avenue, Middelharnis**, Meyndert Hobbema (1638–1709), the National Gallery, London

9. **The Milkmaid**, Jan Vermeer (1632–75), Rijksmuseum, Amsterdam

10. **Flowers in a Vase**, Rachel Ruysch (1664–1750), the National Gallery, London

11. **Madame de Pompadour**, François Boucher (1703–70), Alte Pinakothek, Munich

12. **The Turnip Scraper**, Jean-Baptiste-Siméon Chardin (1699–1779), National Gallery of Art, Washington, D.C., Samuel H. Kress Collection

13. **The "Fighting Téméraire" Tugged to Her Last Berth to Be Broken Up, 1838**, Joseph Mallord William Turner (1775–1851), the National Gallery, London

14. **Looking East from the Giudecca: Early Morning,** Joseph Mallord William Turner, the British Museum, London

15. **Ophelia**, John Everett Millais (1829–96), Tate Gallery, London

16. **Ophelia Among the Flowers**, Odilon Redon (1840–1916), the National Gallery, London

17. **In the Dining Room**, Berthe Morisot (1841–95), National Gallery of Art, Washington, D.C., Chester Dale Collection

18. **The Seine at Asnières (The Skiff)**, Pierre-Auguste Renoir (1841–1919), the National Gallery, London

19. **La La at the Cirque Fernando, Paris**, Hilaire-Germain-Edgar Degas (1834–1917), the National Gallery, London

20. **Self-portrait**, Vincent van Gogh (1853–90), Musée d'Orsay, Paris

21. **Weeping Woman**, Pablo Picasso (1881–1973), Tate Gallery, London

22. **The Horde**, Max Ernst (1891–1976), Stedelijk Museum, Amsterdam

23. **The Persistence of Memory**, Salvador Dali (1904–89), the Museum of Modern Art, New York

24. **Blue Poles: Number II**, Jackson Pollock (1912–56), Australian National Gallery, Canberra

INDEX

Abstract painting, 32, 33, 34

Action painting, 32

Altarpiece, 10, 11, 25, 34, 35, 36

Boucher, François, 20, 21, 36

Campin, Robert, 10, 11, 36

Chardin, Jean-Baptiste-Siméon, 21, 36

Dali, Salvador, 31, 36

Degas, Hilaire-Germain-Edgar, 27, 36

Double portrait, 16, 34

Easel, 8, 24, 34

Ernst, Max, 30, 36

Fresco, 12, 13, 34

Greece, Ancient, 8, 34, 35

Greeks, Ancient, 14

Hobbema, Meyndert, 18, 36

Illuminations, 8, 34

Impressionists, 7, 26, 27, 28

Michelangelo, 12, 13, 36

Millais, John Everett, 24, 25, 36

Morisot, Berthe, 7, 26, 27, 36

Palette, 8, 34

Picasso, Pablo, 29, 36

Pollock, Jackson, 32, 33, 36

Portrait, 6, 16, 17, 20, 28, 35

Pre-Raphaelite Brotherhood, 25

Raphael, 25

Redon, Odilon, 25, 36

Rembrandt, 17, 36

Renaissance, 12, 13, 14, 35

Renoir, Pierre-Auguste, 26, 27, 36

Rome, Ancient, 34, 35

Rubens, Peter Paul, 6, 16, 17, 36

Ruysch, Rachel, 7, 19, 36

Self-portrait, 11, 16, 17, 28, 35, 36

Sistine Chapel, 12

Still life, 18, 35

Studio, 13, 27, 35

Surrealism, 30

Surrealists, 30, 31, 32

Titian, 14, 36

Turner, Joseph Mallord William, 22, 23, 36

Van Gogh, Vincent, 28, 29, 32, 36

Vermeer, Jan, 18, 19, 26, 36

Watercolor, 23, 35

The Author's and Publishers' thanks are due to the following for permission to reproduce photographs:

r = right, *l* = left

Alte Pinakothek, Munich: 16, 20; Australian National Gallery, Canberra: 32; Bibliothèque Nationale, Paris: 9; Trustees of the British Museum: 13; the Metropolitan Museum of Art, New York: 11; Musées Nationaux, Paris: 28; the Musem of Modern Art, New York: 31; Trustees of the National Gallery, London: 17, 18 *l*, 19, 22, 25, 26*r*, 27; National Gallery of Art, Washington, D.C.: 21, 26l; National Gallery of Scotland, Edinburgh: 15; Rijksmuseum, Amsterdam: 18 *r*; Scala Istituto Fotografico: 12; Stedelijk Museum, Amsterdam: 30; Tate Gallery, London: 24, 29, cover; the Turner Collection, Tate Gallery, London: 23.

Cover illustration: **The Cholmondeley Sisters** (artist unknown)